BEGINNING HISTORY

THE
AMERICAN
WEST

Lucy Williams

Illustrated by Peter Dennis

BEGINNING HISTORY

All words that appear in **bold** are explained in the glossary on page 22.

Series Editor: Deborah Elliott
Book Editor: James Kerr
Designer: Helen White

First published in 1991 by Wayland (Publishers) Limited, 61 Western Road,
Hove, East Sussex BN3 1JD

British Library Cataloguing in Publication Data
Williams, Lucy
The American West
1. United States. Western states, to 1899
I. Title   II. Series
978.01

ISBN 0–7502–0057–X

Typeset by Kalligraphic Design Limited, Horley, Surrey.
Printed in Italy by G. Canale & C.s.p.A., Turin.
Bound in Belgium by Casterman, S.A.

CONTENTS

THE FIRST SETTLERS

The first Europeans to arrive in America were the Spanish. In 1607, about 100 English people sailed to the new land. They claimed it as their own and called it Virginia. Soon after, other British settlers joined them. Many of them sailed to America to escape from enemies in Britain.

Life was hard. The settlers stayed at the edge of the country, on the East coast, and lived in log cabins. To the west was a range of high mountains called the Appalachians. The settlers did not know what was on the other side.

THE NATIVE AMERICANS

Before the settlers arrived, over 600 tribes of Native Americans lived in America. The Europeans called them Indians. Some, like the Sioux, were **nomads** and hunters. Others farmed and lived in villages.

The Europeans fought wars with the Native Americans and moved them off their land. The tribes wanted to stay on their sacred

Above *A Native American chief.*

Below *Sioux and Apaches.*

hunting grounds. When they were forced out, many of them died of European diseases.

The tribes of the Great Plains rode horses and hunted buffalo. As settlers moved across their land, herds of buffalo were wiped out.

EXPLORERS AND TRAPPERS

Small bands of explorers went across America. Adventurers followed them, like Daniel Boone, who from 1769 stayed in the forest for two years. These adventurers found many new kinds of animals and plants.

They stayed in the wild, and lived by trapping beavers and trading animal skins.

They lived all year round in the country, and did not build towns. They married and traded with Native Americans, and wore **buckskin** clothes. Once a year they all met up to have a party and send their goods east by pack-horses.

Below *Kit Carson, a famous explorer of the American West.*

Above *A painting of Daniel Boone.*

9

WAGON TRAINS

From the 1780s onwards, thousands of **pioneers** went west to seek a new life. They loaded food, clothes and bedding on to covered wagons pulled by oxen, and set off in search of land to farm.

Life was dangerous on the western trails. Many pioneers died from diseases and hunger. The Native

Americans sometimes attacked them with bows and arrows, and pioneers had to wheel the wagons into a circle and hide inside.

The government had to build **stockades** along the way, to protect the pioneers.

LIFE ON THE LAND

The first land the pioneers came to was wooded. Some stayed, cleared the forest and lived in log cabins. They grew vegetables such as sweet corn and potatoes.

In the middle of America stretched enormous grassy **prairies**. Slowly the settlers claimed the land. When there was no timber to build with, they cut lumps of turf from the ground and made **sod** houses. They used windmills to pump water.

The settlers had to survive **cyclones**, dust storms, blizzards and plagues of grasshoppers. But they were determined to stay on the land they had claimed.

GOLD IN THE HILLS!

Below *Miners in California, painted in 1851.*

Explorers saw some shiny flakes at the bottom of a stream in the mountains of California in 1848.

Right *The main street of a gold town.*

When the news spread that the flakes were real gold, people rushed there from all over the world. Some made fortunes by **panning** for gold dust and **nuggets** in the streams.

Tent cities and towns quickly grew up around the new gold mines. Fights often started over who owned the land. When the gold ran out, the **prospectors** moved on. The towns they left behind became **ghost towns**.

COWBOYS AND CATTLE

The grassy wilderness of the West was good for farming cattle. They were branded with a mark and allowed to roam free, and cowboys on horses rounded them up when they

were ready to be sold. Sometimes the cowboys would steal unmarked cattle – this was called rustling.

Frontier towns sprang up, with saloons and hotels. At first there were no laws and the cowboys often had gunfights. Sheriffs had to try to keep the peace.

Some cowboys became outlaws, like Billy the Kid, and lived on the run. They robbed banks and stole cattle for a living.

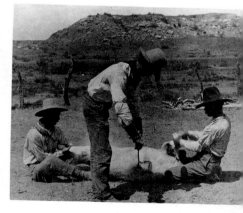

Top *Cowboys rounding up cattle.*

Bottom *Branding cattle.*

WOMEN OF THE WEST

Frontier women had to learn new skills so that their families could survive in the new land. They learned from the Native Americans how to make medicines from herbs and plants, and clothes from **hide**.

Top *A pioneer woman carrying dried cattle manure, used for fuel.*

Bottom *A pioneer woman.*

They looked after children on the trek west, and kept diaries of the long journey. These show people today how hard their lives were. They learned how to use guns to protect themselves.

Arriving in the new towns, women helped set up schools and churches.

How the West was Won

At first, America was the Native Americans' country. But the Europeans destroyed the Native American way of life. Although the tribes fought back with bows and arrows, these were no match for guns. Many of them died from common European diseases, such as influenza.

The settlers built railways and roads across the vast country, and brought in modern machinery to farm their new land. Towns and then cities were built, and a new nation was born.

GLOSSARY

Buckskin The skin of a deer.

Cyclones Dangerous whirlwinds.

Frontier The edge of the settled area of a country.

Ghost towns Deserted towns.

Hide Animal skin.

Nomads People who do not live in one place, but travel around.

Nuggets Small lumps of gold or silver.

Panning Washing gravel in a pan to separate gold from the gravel.

Pioneers People who settle on new land.

Prairies The treeless grassy lands of the central USA and southern Canada.

Prospectors People who search for gold.

Sod Turf.

Stockades Forts for soldiers.

BOOKS TO READ

Daniel Boone and the American West by Robin May (Wayland, 1985)

The American West by Miriam Moss (Wayland, 1986)

The American West by Robin May (Macmillan Children's Books, 1982)

The North American Indians by Anne Steel (Wayland, 1987)

Picture acknowledgements

The publishers would like to thank the following for providing the photographs in this book: Peter Newark's Western Americana 6 (top), 9 (top and bottom), 14 (top and bottom), 17 (top), 19 (top and bottom); Topham 6 (bottom), 17 (bottom).

INDEX